W9-ACH-183

MY DIGITAL HEALTH AND WELLNESS

BEN HUBBARD

ILLUSTRATED BY DIEGO VAISBERG

Lerner Publications ◆ Minneapolis

First American edition published in 2019
by Lerner Publishing Group, Inc.

First published in Great Britain in 2018 by
The Watts Publishing Group
Copyright © The Watts Publishing
Group 2018

Credits
Series Editor: Julia Bird
Illustrator: Diego Vaisberg
Packaged by: Collaborate

Lerner Publications Company
A division of Lerner Publishing Group, Inc.
241 First Avenue North
Minneapolis, MN 55401 USA

For reading levels and more information, look up this title at www.
lernerbooks.com.

Main body text set in Courier PS Std.
Typeface provided by Monotype Typography.

Library of Congress Cataloging-in-Publication Data

The Cataloging-in-Publication Data for *My Digital Health and Wellness*
is on file at the Library of Congress.
ISBN 978-1-5415-3880-1 (lib. bdg.)
ISBN 978-1-5415-4307-2 (eb pdf)

Manufactured in the United States of America
1-45063-35890-7/17/2018

CONTENTS

What Is Digital Citizenship?   4

Your Digital Health and Wellness   6

Prepare to Prevent Pain   8

Stretch, Don't Strain   10

Digital Training   12

App Attack   14

Online Time Limits   16

Online Addiction   18

Social Media and Self-Image   20

Avoiding Ads   22

Being Boys and Girls   24

Digital Detox   26

Digital Quiz   28

Glossary   30

Helpful Websites   31

Index   32

WHAT IS DIGITAL CITIZENSHIP?

When we log onto the internet, we become part of a giant online world. In this world we can use our phones, tablets, and computers to explore, create, and communicate with billions of different people.

Together, these people make up a global digital community. That is why they are known as digital citizens. When you use the internet you become a digital citizen too. So what does this mean?

CITIZEN VS DIGITAL CITIZEN

A good citizen is someone who behaves well, looks after themselves and others, and tries to make their community a better place. A good digital citizen acts exactly the same way. However, the online world is bigger than just a local neighborhood, city, or country. It spans the whole world and crosses every kind of border. It is therefore up to all digital citizens everywhere to make this digital community a safe, fun, and exciting place for everyone.

MY DIGITAL HEALTH AND WELLNESS

It's easy to get wrapped up in the online world. While we explore the internet, play games, or update our social media accounts, hours can pass by without us noticing. Sometimes this can leave our bodies stiff and sore. At other times, what we see online can make us unhappy.

But despite this, we may find it hard to stay away from the internet. However, clever digital citizens learn to balance their online time with looking after their minds and bodies. This book will help you with your digital health and wellness.

WHAT ARE YOU DOING?

JUGGLING MY DIGITAL HEALTH AND WELLNESS AND BRINGING BALANCE TO MY ONLINE LIFE.

WHAT WILL YOU DO WITH THE FRUIT?

JUICE IT DURING MY NEXT MICRO-BREAK.

YOUR DIGITAL HEALTH AND WELLNESS

No one would embark on a real-life adventure without being properly prepared. The online world is the same.

Therefore, digital citizens get ready for going online in two ways: mentally and physically. This is how they protect themselves from harm.

PREPARE PHYSICALLY

Being online is not like running a marathon, but it can still be hard on your body! People who work long hours on digital devices can suffer from pain in their hands, arms, back, and neck. Often this pain can lead to a serious condition called repetitive strain injury, or RSI (see page 8). However, RSI and other similar conditions are easy to prevent. You can keep yourself pain free by preparing physically to go online and then paying attention to your body.

When we are online it can sometimes seem like our brains are hardwired into the internet. We may feel like multitasking wizards who can juggle messaging, exploring websites, and playing games all at once. Sometimes we are so focused on the screen that many hours simply slip away. Afterward we can feel a little burned out. It may be hard to concentrate on other tasks, but we can't wait to be back online.

However, we all need to give our brains a digital break now and then. This helps us digest what we've seen in the online world and to remind ourselves it is not the same as the real world.

PREPARE TO PREVENT PAIN

The human body has evolved over hundreds of thousands of years to carry out physical tasks.

We were not designed for sitting in front of a computer making small, repetitive movements for hours on end. To perform this relatively new work, we must look after our bodies and help them adjust.

REPETITIVE STRAIN INJURY

A repetitive strain injury is a painful condition that usually affects the hands, wrists, and arms. It is caused by repeating small movements over and over again, and it therefore often affects computer users. Its symptoms include stiffness, tingling, numbness, and burning sensations. It's important that if you feel any of these symptoms you limit using your digital devices and talk to a doctor as soon as possible. Repetitive strain injuries are treatable, but it's best to prevent them from happening in the first place.

SITTING STRAIGHT

How we sit at a computer is the first step in preventing pain and physical problems. Follow these five easy steps to set up your work station correctly:

1 Support your back with a chair that keeps your spine straight and not hunched. This is called good posture.

2 Position the screen to eye level so you are not bending your neck to look at it.

MY WRISTS ARE KILLING ME!

NO WONDER! LOOK AT HOW YOU'RE SITTING! TAKE A BREAK AND THEN I'LL HELP YOU SET UP A PROPER WORK STATION.

3 Keep your legs bent at a right angle, with your feet flat on a footrest or the ground.

4 Keep your arms at a right angle to the desk, so you are not reaching up or down to type.

5 Make sure your hands and wrists are straight and not bent while using the keyboard and mouse.

STRETCH, DON'T STRAIN

Have you ever noticed how you hold your body when you are concentrating on something online? Often we make our limbs rigid, hunch up our shoulders, and even clench our jaws. Without even realizing it we are making ourselves tense and tight. This is very bad for our bodies. Clever digital citizens take micro-breaks to stretch their muscles and relax.

BREAK AND STRETCH

Taking a five-minute micro-break every twenty minutes can help relieve stiffness and tension and prevent pain in the future. During your break, try these six stretches. They may seem funny at first, but you'll feel great after doing them!

1 Stretch your fingers out straight, hold for ten seconds, then relax. Now bend your fingers at the knuckles, hold for ten seconds, then relax.

2 Raise your eyebrows, open your eyes and mouth wide and stick out your tongue for ten seconds. Try not to laugh. Then relax.

3 Raise your shoulders slowly up to your ears, hold for five seconds, then relax.

AVOID EYESTRAIN

With all that time spent staring at screens, digital citizens need to look after their eye health. A simple exercise is to look away from the screen every twenty minutes and concentrate on something in the distance for twenty seconds or so. This helps relax the eye muscles and prevent eyestrain. Also remember to blink often!

WHAT ARE YOU DOING?

YOGA. WE'RE PREPARING FOR A HARDCORE GAMING SESSION.

4 Lock your fingers behind your head and pull your shoulder blades gently together. Hold for ten seconds, then relax.

5 Slowly tilt your head to one side, hold for ten seconds, then straighten and relax. Now do the same on the other side.

6 Slowly turn your chin toward your left shoulder, hold for ten seconds, then relax. Now do the same for the other side.

DIGITAL TRAINING

Has an adult ever told you that a healthy body leads to a healthy mind?

It may sound boring, but it is actually true. Smart digital citizens train to be online by doing some physical exercise every day and getting enough sleep. This keeps their brains sharp and their bodies in shape for every internet adventure.

WHAT IS THAT?

HEALTHY DIGITAL CITIZENS

In the late twentieth century, doctors realized people were spending too much time sitting in front of screens. As a result, they were becoming unfit and prone to health problems. Now, it is understood that children need to exercise for at least 60 minutes a day to stay healthy.

EXERCISE NOW

It's easy to put off doing exercise when you are online. There's always a message to finish, a website to browse, or a level to conquer. Before you know it, it's time to have dinner or go to bed. But it's also easy to stand up and do some exercise, such as run, ride a bike, or walk. Setting an alarm is a good way to remind yourself to do this.

IT'S A WAY OF EXERCISING AND STAYING ONLINE AT THE SAME TIME. IT SHUTS DOWN EVERY 20 MINUTES SO I'M FORCED TO TAKE A MICRO-BREAK.

SWITCH OFF BEFORE SLEEP

Did you know that staring at a screen before bedtime is like running a race and then trying to sleep? Turning all your digital devices off at least an hour before bedtime is the best way of winding down and getting a proper night's rest. The online world will still be there in the morning.

APP ATTACK

Twenty years ago, people mainly sat at desktop computers to go online.

Back then, the internet was brand new and some people said it would never catch on! Now, the internet is part of everyday life and our smartphones keep us constantly connected wherever we go. These digital devices can make us feel in control—but are they controlling us? Smart digital citizens look after their mental health as much as their physical health.

PICK UP THAT PHONE?

Do you ever find yourself picking up your smartphone without realizing? It's a great tool to have around, but it's also something to look at when you don't know what else to do. How much time do you spend randomly picking up your phone? Why not try a diary experiment? For one day, write down each time you pick up your phone, and record how long you use it for and what you do on it. When you look at the results, ask yourself: "How much of this time was well spent?"

THE ANTI APPS

If you think you are picking up your digital device too often, you could try one of the following activities. These "Anti Apps" will help you fill your time differently.

1 Write a letter. Use a pen and paper and send the letter in an envelope. Your gran will be amazed!

2 Draw a picture. Use pens, pencils, and paper and don't check the internet for inspiration.

I FEEL AWFUL!

Sometimes being online can make us feel confused, anxious, or depressed. We can see things that upset us or read things that make us feel bad about ourselves. Looking after your mental health is a very important aspect of being a digital citizen. If you are experiencing any of the things listed above, then it's important to talk to someone. Your trusted adult is a great place to start. There are also phone helplines where you can talk to experts anonymously. Most of all, this is a good time to take a break from the online world.

AT 11:37 AM YOU LOOKED AT YOUR WEATHER APP FOR 53 SECONDS. THEN AT 11:39 AM YOU LOOKED AT IT AGAIN. WHY?

SEE? IT POPS RIGHT BACK INTO MY HAND. I THOUGHT IT WAS COOL, BUT NOW IT WON'T LEAVE ME ALONE. PLEASE GET IT OFF!

I DON'T KNOW. I THOUGHT IT MIGHT RAIN.

3 Listen to the radio. Try the news, talk shows, or music for a different method of getting information. Only 100 years ago, people did this instead of watching TV!

4 Read a book to relax or learn something new. There are so many different types of books, everyone can find some they like.

ONLINE TIME LIMITS

Did you ever sit down for a five-minute gaming session just to find that five hours had passed?

You wanted to stop—but only after you reached the end of the level. It's always easy to find an excuse to stay online, but clever digital citizens know when and how to take a break.

> ▶▶▶▶▶▶▶▶▶▶▶▶▶▶
>
> CONGRATULATIONS
> PLAYER,
> LEVEL 38 CRACKED!

> SAM, ONLY 20 MORE
> MINUTES, OK?

> YES, YES,
> FINE, FINE.

MAKING TIME

All digital citizens know, there's never quite enough time to fit everything into a day. There are too many social media posts to make, messages to write, websites to visit, and gaming worlds to explore. Then there is the real world too! The best way to divide your time between the real world and online world is to set an alarm. When it rings, your online time is up. Walk away!

GAMING DANGER

Online gaming is a bit like a social network where you can connect with other players. Players often "trash talk" each other, but you must be careful of what you say. Sometimes a player's comments can become abusive and turn into a type of cyberbullying. If another player upsets you, make sure to walk away and tell your trusted adult.

ONLINE ADDICTION

For some digital citizens, spending too much time online leads to more serious problems.

They can become addicted to the digital world and find it difficult to do anything else. Sometimes, they give up seeing other people and become isolated and alone. When this happens, they often need help to get better.

MADDY? WE'D LIKE TO TALK TO YOU.

MADDY'S ROOM

GO AWAY!

I HAVEN'T SEEN YOU IN DAYS!

AM I ADDICTED?

There is a big difference between spending lots of time online and being addicted. However, if you experience the following signs it is best to talk to your trusted adult about it:

1 You spend all of your spare time online and sacrifice sleep to be on it.

2 You become angry, irritated, or depressed when you are not online.

THE REWARD FEELING

The online world can make us feel good in lots of ways. On social media, we look forward to receiving comments about our posts and then feel rewarded when people "like" them. Finishing a difficult level in an online game can feel rewarding too. Some people want to feel the excitement the internet provides over and over again, until they become addicted to it.

MAD
ROO

GO AW

I DON'T KNOW WHAT TO DO. I CAN'T STOP GAMING.

THAT'S OK, WE CAN HELP YOU.

3 You disobey time limits set for being online and lie about it.

4 You prefer to be online than spend time with friends or family.

5 Your school work is suffering and you ignore other commitments to be online.

SOCIAL MEDIA AND SELF-IMAGE

Social media is one of our favorite ways to stay in touch with friends and family.

With our smartphones we can instantly snap a selfie and upload it in seconds. While we wait for comments, we can check out what our friends have posted too. However, sometimes this can make us feel bad about ourselves. It can seem like other people have more friends and are having a better time than us.

MALCOLM HAS OVER 150 FRIENDS AND ALWAYS SEEMS TO BE HAVING FUN.

LIKE THE HUMAN

Often the best social media posts are of people looking silly, making a mistake, or laughing at themselves. This is because they are celebrating being human and sharing it with others. This is much more fun than posting perfect photos or writing about our exciting lives. So the next time you slip over or spill soup down your front, post a picture of it and see what kind of responses come in.

BEST FACE FORWARD

Clever digital citizens remember that social media is not a true reflection of the real world. That is because most people only post pictures of themselves looking good— and some retouch or digitally alter the photos first. The same is often true of people's activities. Some people's social media accounts make their lives seem action-packed and amazing. But that's because nobody posts images of themselves getting up in the morning or tying their shoelaces. It's important to remember that nobody's life is always interesting or without problems.

JAMES HAS MUCH BETTER FRIENDS THAN ME AND IS ALWAYS DOING COOL STUFF WITH THEM.

AVOIDING ADS

Have you ever noticed how many advertisements there are online?

Ads are crammed into every nook and cranny, flashing and popping up at us and enticing us to click on them. They promise us beauty, success, and happiness if we buy their products. However, clever digital citizens know not to believe them.

PLEASE, IT'S THE LATEST THING. I NEED IT!

OK, BUT THIS WILL BE YOUR BIRTHDAY PRESENT.

ADS AND MARKETING

Marketing is how ads target particular groups to sell them things. That is why many ads are aimed at kids. Marketers often call children under the age of 12 "pesterers." This is because they don't have much money of their own but often pester their parents to buy them the "latest thing." Marketers promise the latest thing will make us happy, but the latest thing is soon replaced by another latest thing. Smart digital citizens know that buying products can bring a few moments of pleasure, but it cannot provide us with long-term happiness.

NOT NEWS

Have you ever clicked on a news story online just to find out it is actually an advertisement? This is one way clever advertisers trick us into reading about their products. Sometimes these ads in disguise are labeled "sponsored content," "promoted," or "advertisement." However, when they are not labeled, we need to keep our wits about us and pause before clicking on them.

CHECK THIS OUT, IT'S THE LATEST THING!

NO, THAT STOPPED BEING THE LATEST THING YESTERDAY AFTERNOON. THIS IS NOW THE LATEST THING!

BEING BOYS AND GIRLS

The online world is full of images and advice about how we should look and act as girls and boys.

These are known as gender stereotypes. Gender stereotypes often tell us that girls should be pretty, polite, and ladylike, while boys should be tough, athletic, and never cry. Smart digital citizens do not buy into gender stereotypes. Instead they promote an equal online world where people are allowed to be themselves.

WOAH. LOOK AT THAT GUY. I WISH I WERE LIKE HIM.

SHE LOOKS SO PERFECT!

THE MALE AND FEMALE MODEL

Online ads, celebrity websites, and fashion e-zines like to show us models with toned bodies and perfect smiles and hair. These can make us feel bad about the way we look. However, it's important to remember these images have nothing to do with the real world. Most people do not look like models, and many online photos of models have been heavily retouched and digitally altered before being published.

BREAK THE MOLD

The online world shows us many gender stereotypes, but it is also a great place to fight against them. For example, boys and girls can use male or female avatars and screen names or choose ones that are unisex. It is also a great place to educate people that stereotypes make the world a more narrow-minded place. After all, there are lots of athletic girls and polite boys, and everyone is allowed to cry!

YEAH BUT LOOK, I FOUND THE UNALTERED VERSION. THIS IS WHAT THEY REALLY LOOK LIKE!

DIGITAL TOLERANCE

Good digital citizens believe in a tolerant world where people can be what they want. This includes boys who like dressing as girls. It can also include girls and boys who feel like they were born as the wrong gender and want to swap. Called the transgender community, these people have a big presence on the internet. This helps others understand who they are and helps to eliminate prejudices people may have against them.

DIGITAL DETOX

The online world is a fast-moving place that never sleeps.

You can have instant communication with others, play games around the clock, and browse websites at any time of day or night. No wonder that digital citizens can feel a little frazzled at times. When you feel like this, it's a good idea to give yourself a digital detox.

SORRY, I'M READING MY BOOK.

DO YOU KNOW WHAT THE WI-FI LOG IN IS HERE?

TURN OFF AND TUNE IN

Taking a digital detox means switching off all your devices and giving your brain a break. This is a great time to visit a friend in person. It helps you remember real humans are fun, friendly, and have flaws, unlike the edited versions they can post on their social media accounts.

FANTASY VS REALITY

Online gaming is great entertainment, but sometimes it can be hard to shake a game off. If you find yourself walking down a street imagining jumping over cars, hurling grenades, or driving rally cars, perhaps you are suffering from gaming overload. Thankfully, the real world is a much calmer and more ordered place. Remember to enjoy it too.

NON DIGITAL CITIZENS

When we're online, it's easy to imagine that the whole world is online too. But it isn't. There are billions of people in the world who don't have a digital device or an internet connection. Many of them live around us. It's nice to remember that being a digital citizen is not essential to having a fulfilling life. After all, the greatest experiences in life happen in the real world, not the online one.

DIGITAL QUIZ

Now that you've reached the end of this book, how do you feel about your digital health and wellness? How much have you learned? And how much can you remember? Take this quiz and tally up your score at the end to find out.

1. What is an injury that can be caused by too much computer use?
a. Repetitive stain injury
b. Repetitive strain injury
c. Repetitive pain injury

2. How should our feet best be positioned while using a computer at a desk?
a. Dangling
b. Stretched out on a beanbag
c. Flat on the floor

3. How long should a micro-break last?
a. Around 5 minutes
b. 2 minutes and 45 seconds
c. 20 minutes

4. What should you NOT do to get a good night's sleep?
a. Play online games in bed
b. Check your social media account before switching off the light
c. Turn off all digital devices at least an hour before bedtime

5. Which could be a sign you are addicted to the internet?
a. You have glued your smartphone to your hand
b. You become angry, irritated, or depressed when you are not online
c. Your sister said so

6. Set ideas about how boys and girls should look and behave are called...
a. Member stereotypes
b. Remember stereotypes
c. Gender stereotypes

7. How many people in the world are there without an internet connection?

a. 378

b. 3 million

c. Billions

8. What is a digital detox?

a. A type of fruit drink that harnesses the power of bananas

b. Taking time off being online

c. A diet that your mom mentioned once

HOW DID YOU DO? ADD UP YOUR SCORE TO SEE.

1-4: You are on your way, but retake the quiz to get a score over 4.

5-7: You've passed the quiz well. Now see if you can pass the quiz in the book *My Digital Safety and Security*.

8: Wow! 8 out of 8. You are a natural born digital citizen!

29

GLOSSARY

addiction
Feeling physically and mentally dependent on having something

apps
Short for "applications," apps are computer programs for mobile digital devices, such as smartphones or tablets.

avatar
A computer icon or image that people use to represent themselves online

detox
Taking a break from something that is done often and may have harmful effects

digital
Technology that involves computers

internet
The vast electronic network that allows billions of computers from around the world to connect to each other

online
Being connected to the internet via a computer or digital device

selfie
Taking a photo of oneself, often using a smartphone

smartphone
A mobile phone that is capable of connecting to the internet

social media
Websites that allow users to share content and information online

stereotype
An oversimplified view of somebody held by many people

trusted adult
An adult you know well and trust who can help you with all issues relating to the internet

unisex
Something that can be used by people of any gender

upload
Transferring something from your computer or digital device onto the internet

website
A collection of web pages that is stored on a computer and made available to people over the internet

HELPFUL WEBSITES

Digital Citizenship
The following websites have helpful information about digital citizenship for young people:

http://www.digizen.org/kids

http://www.digitalcitizenship
.nsw.edu.au/Prim_Splash/

http://www.cyberwise.org
/digital-citizenship-games

Bullying
These websites have excellent advice for kids who are experiencing bullying online:

https://www.childline.org.uk
/info-advice/bullying-abuse
-safety/types-bullying/online
-bullying/

http://www.bullying.co.uk

https://www.stopbullying.gov
/kids/facts/

Staying Safe
These websites are dedicated to keeping kids safe online, with lots of good advice:

http://www.childnet.com/young
-people/primary

http://www.kidsmart.org.uk

http://www.safetynetkids.org.uk
/personal-safety/staying-safe
-online/

http://www.bbc.co.uk
/newsround/13910067

INDEX

addiction, 18–19
ads, 22–24
alarms, 13, 16

breaks, digital,
    7, 10–11, 13–
    17, 26–27

computer set up,
    8–9
cyberbullying, 17

detox, digital,
    26–27

exercise, 12–13
exercises,
    stretching,
    10–11
eyestrain, 11

feeling, reward,
    19

gaming, online,
    5, 7, 16–17,
    19, 26–27
gender, 24–25

health, caring
    for mental, 7,
    14–25
health, caring
    for physical,
    6–14

marketing, 22–23
micro-breaks, 5,
    10–11, 13

posture, 8–9

repetitive strain
    injury (RSI),
    6, 8

self-image, 20–
    21, 24
selfies, 20–21
sitting
    (correctly),
    8–9
sleep, 13, 18
smartphones, 4,
    14–15, 20
social media, 5,
    16, 19–21, 26,
    28
stereotypes,
    gender, 24–25

time limits,
    16–17